NO PLACE LIKE HOME

NO PLACE LIKE HOME

Text by Claire Berrisford

An Hachette UK Company
www.hachette.co.uk

Vie Books, an imprint of Summersdale Publishers Ltd
Part of Octopus Publishing Group Limited
Carmelite House
50 Victoria Embankment
LONDON
EC4Y 0DZ
UK

www.summersdale.com

Printed and bound in the Czech Republic

ISBN: 978-1-80007-019-6

Substantial discounts on bulk quantities of Summersdale books are available to corporations, professional associations and other organizations. For details contact general enquiries: telephone: +44 (0) 1243 771107 or email: enquiries@summersdale.com.

NO PLACE LIKE HOME

The Mindful Way to a Healthy and Happy Home Life

Jo Peters

Where we love is home,
home that our feet may
leave, but not our hearts.

Oliver Wendell Holmes Sr

CONTENTS

What makes a house a home?

There's no place like home. It's where we go to relax at the end of a busy day. It's where we shelter and recharge, and, most importantly, it should be where we feel happiest.

When the pandemic disrupted the normal pattern of our days, it shed light on the things in life that really matter. As such, our relationship toward our homes shifted. "Home" is not merely a base for eating and sleeping – it's a part of who we are and it has a huge effect on our mental health, our well-being and our outlook on life. For many people, home is now also a workplace and we now spend more time indoors than we do outside – so it's more important than ever to ensure that the place we live is somewhere that brings us joy and comfort.

This book will show you how to bring out the best in your home. Wherever you live and whatever your budget, there are myriad ways to make your home into a haven that fosters happiness and mental well-being. Find tips on bringing the outside in, discover ways to create your own private space for creativity and calm, learn how to make your workspace healthy and productive, enjoy recipes for comfort food, indoor picnics and coffee-shop favourites, and find solace in a collection of beautiful quotes and poetry. Most of all, settle into this book to be soothed, refreshed and inspired to truly make your house into your home.

HOME SANCTUARY

Coming home is something we should all look forward to, like the warm open arms of a hug. In our homes we should feel safe, secure and happy. From personalizing your space to decluttering, this chapter will point you toward ideas to help you refresh your home so that it's a true sanctuary.

A HAPPY HOME

Does the colour of your walls matter? How important is the choice of one style of chair over another? Is spending time, effort and money on the interior of your home really worth it?

We all react to spaces, even though we may not be aware of it. It's what makes you feel at home in some places and uneasy in others. If you have ever house-hunted before, you'll know that – for some reason you may not be able to explain – some places give you a spark of warmth and joy, and others leave you cold. This is because our subconscious picks up on tiny details about a space independently from our conscious minds. This was demonstrated in a 2019 experiment* in neuroaesthetics (how our brain responds to the things we see), which saw participants walking through three differently designed rooms, wearing a device that could track their body's response. They were then asked to detail their thoughts on each room. The findings showed that the participants didn't necessarily feel calmest in their favourite design aesthetic. In other words, a person's body and subconscious acted independently of their conscious thoughts.

So, the answer is "yes". The design of a space isn't superficial or trivial – it really matters. Not only is it a way to express your personality and sense of style, but taking control of your home is a way to look after your mental health and well-being – because the right room has the ability to put the deepest part of your mind at ease.

When you have some time alone at home, walk around each room. Do this in silence without any distractions and take your time. Spend a while in each room and think about how you feel. What is your state of mind like? Is it racing or calm? How does it feel in your body? Do your answers match up with how you would like to feel in these rooms?

* www.wallpaper.com

BE INSPIRED BY FENG SHUI

For thousands of years, there has been a correlation between our homes and our health and well-being. The ancient Chinese practice of Feng Shui is a reflection of this and still informs interior design today. It's based on the concept of *qi* (pronounced "chee"), the energy of the world, which moves through the five elements – fire, earth, metal, water and wood – and is the art of designing your home so that the Earth's life force can flow freely. The home is divided into a grid of nine squares. (The same grid can apply to a room too.)

WEALTH AND PROSPERITY
SOUTH-EAST
Purple.
Wood element.

FAME AND REPUTATION
SOUTH
Red.
Fire element.

RELATIONSHIPS
SOUTH-WEST
Pink.
Earth element.

FAMILY
EAST
Green.
Wood element.

HEALTH
CENTRE
Yellow.
Earth element.

CHILDREN AND CREATIVITY
WEST
White.
Metal element.

KNOWLEDGE AND SELF-CULTIVATION
NORTH-WEST
Blue.
Earth element.

CAREER
NORTH
Black.
Water element.

TRAVEL AND HELPFUL PEOPLE
NORTH-EAST
Grey.
Metal element.

Here are some ways that you can apply the practice to your own home to encourage balance, good health, love and prosperity:

- Find the commanding position of a room, and try placing larger pieces of furniture there, such as beds or desks. The commanding position is usually the spot furthest away from the door that's not directly in line with it – although the door should be visible from the spot. This position is a place of power within the room.

- If you have a flight of stairs directly in front of the door, add something to your entranceway to give yourself and your guests a pause, such as a mirror on the wall, art or an ornament. This keeps you in the moment and prevents your eye from being immediately drawn away and up the stairs.

- Keep your rooms tidy and free of clutter, as this helps you to retain mental clarity. You can find more tips on how to do this on page 24.

- Keep pathways and entrances clear, so that energy can flow through your home. In practice, make sure walkways don't contain tripping hazards and avoid putting a large piece of furniture in the direct line of a doorway.

- Include the five elements – earth, metal, fire, wood and water – in each room. You can be literal or metaphorical with this. For instance, for earth you could include crystals, terracotta items, or earthy tones; for water you could have a real water feature or cool, watery colours, flowing shapes and materials, or a mirror.

COLOUR YOURSELF HAPPY

Colour therapy is the practice of using colour to influence how you think and feel. It is a technique that's been used to help people manage anxiety and boost confidence, as well as cultivate positivity and well-being.

First, think about your home. What does it look like and what colours is it filled with? Next, think about the colours that you're drawn to. Do you like bright pops of colour or calming pastels? Muted shades or clashing ones? If the colours you like aren't the same as the colours you're surrounded by, it might be time to get creative.

If you're nervous about adding colour, start small. Choose just one room to work on and bring in a few colourful items at a time so you can play around with colours you like. Look up some design inspiration online and create a mood board of the things you are drawn to. If you're ready to splash out and get painting, think about the ambience you want to create, or the side of your personality that you want to project. Do you want something that makes you feel cosy or something that makes you feel energized? Do you want the room to feel fun, calming or bold?

If you can't or don't want to paint your walls, there are still plenty of ways to tailor your home to your own sense of style. Bring in colourful fabrics – duvets, cushions, throws and rugs – hang up art and prints with self-adhesive hooks that won't mark your walls, or treat yourself to your favourite colourful flowers that you can display on your table or windowsill.

Your home is a canvas and it's yours to fill with the colours that you love.

COLOUR	MEANING	ROOM
Red	Adventure, passion, courage	Bedroom and living room
Yellow	Energy, happiness, focus	Study, kitchen
Green	Healing, balance, the natural world	Living room and bedroom
Blue	Calm, peace, productivity	Bedroom, study and bathroom
Purple	Creativity, spirituality, calm	Bedroom, living room
Pink	Love, calm, tenderness	Living room and bedroom
Orange	Warmth, sociability, confidence	Living room and bedroom
Black	Strength, elegance, power	Living room and study
White	Purity, cleanliness, peacefulness	Living room, kitchen, study, bathroom

Extract from

MY HOME

This is the place that I love the best,
A little brown house, like a ground-bird's nest,
Hid among grasses, and vines, and trees,
Summer retreat of the birds and bees.

The tenderest light that ever was seen
Sifts through the vine-made window screen—
Sifts and quivers, and flits and falls
On home-made carpets and gray-hung walls.

In the cunningest chamber under the sun
I sink to sleep when the day is done;
And am waked at morn, in my snow-white bed,
By a singing bird on the roof o'erhead.

Better than treasures brought from Rome,
Are the living pictures I see at home—
My aged father, with frosted hair,
And mother's face, like a painting rare.

Far from the city's dust and heat,
I get but sounds and odors sweet.
Who can wonder I love to stay,
Week after week, here hidden away,
In this sly nook that I love the best—
This little brown house like a ground-bird's nest?

Ella Wheeler Wilcox

EXPLORE CRYSTAL HEALING

For generations, humans have been drawn to natural crystals. They vibrate with energy, which is the reason we find them in modern inventions such as lasers and watches. However, these vibrations can also be used for healing. When we are stressed or sad, the vibrations of certain crystals are said to have an effect on our bodies that promotes a renewed sense of calm and well-being. For instance, when kept close or held on your person, pyrite can be used to help inspire confidence, amethyst can alleviate anxiety and aventurine can soothe anger as well as increase your fortune and opportunities.

There are also plenty of uses for crystals around your home. Try the following to promote different energies in your living space:

- **Front door:** Use black tourmaline near the entrance of your home, as this stone is protective and helps to prevent negative energy from entering.

- **Living room:** Use amethyst or amber for a relaxing space, peridot or citrine for a positive one, or aquamarine if you would like to reduce stress.

- **Kitchen:** If you're an enthusiastic cook, choose carnelian for energy, stamina and creativity. To enhance the nurturing energy of the room, choose rose quartz.

- **Study:** Use citrine to help you focus, pyrite to promote ideas and confidence, or shungite to combat the electric energy of computers and other devices.

- **Bathroom:** Use clear quartz, the cleansing stone, to purify your energy as well as your body.

- **Bedroom:** Choose rose quartz to promote feelings of peace and love, or selenite, which is a natural energy cleanser and therefore good for restful sleep.

Don't be afraid to experiment with your own crystal placements too. Think about the energy you want to attract to each room and try out different combinations of crystals to help achieve it.

MANIFEST YOUR GOALS

Manifesting means to bring something into existence through your thoughts, feelings or beliefs. You can manifest a mood, an item or an experience – the key is focusing your attention on the thing that you want, as this is how you draw it toward you.

Allow your home to help you invite positive changes and good things into your life. A technique for manifesting your goals is to regularly meditate on what you want to achieve. Perhaps you want a change in your luck, a new job or you have a specific dream you want to make reality. Write down some positive or inspiring statements, and put these up around your home where you will see them and constantly be reminded of what you are aiming for. For example:

I am loved

or

I am successful

You could even take this one step further and turn your statements into a mood board, which can then provide visual inspiration every day.

Your energy helps to create your reality, so make sure your home is working with you rather than against you; if you want to attract positive things, your energy must be positive. Therefore, ensure that your home reflects this. Decorate it with colours that bring you joy (see page 16) and place things that make you happy, such as photos or trinkets, where you'll see them.

Manifesting desires requires a deep sense of self-awareness and self-belief, so being patient and honest with yourself is key.

THE CATHARTIC
ART OF TIDYING

Most of us feel calmest in our spaces when they're ordered and tidy. Getting to that point can be a daunting prospect, but with the right approach, it needn't be. Decluttering is the mindful way to tidy your home. It's not about throwing everything away or trying to whittle your belongings down to the bare minimum. It simply means taking stock of the things that you have and letting go of anything that is unnecessary. It's a way of making sure that the things you have are the things you use and love – and that you have exactly what you need.

It's a simple activity, but its effects are wide-reaching. Your home is a sanctuary, and having a tidy and organized space can have a hugely positive effect on your mood and your outlook on life. It's also easier to relax in a space that's tidy. The very act of tidying can be therapeutic too; making small but confident decisions about what you do and don't need allows you to check in with yourself and your life, and helps you to feel in control.

Begin by picking one area of your home. It could be a room or even just one drawer. Go through everything you find in that area item by item, and sort each one into the following piles: things to keep, things to throw away and things to rehome. As you sort through, the most important thing is that you're honest with yourself. The phrase "just in case" is a red flag; if you find yourself thinking it, be honest with yourself about whether you really need to keep the item you're considering.

Room to breathe

Not all of us have the luxury of spacious houses – but that doesn't mean that a room can't be made to *feel* big. If you find that your living area is cramped, try some of these techniques to create the illusion of a roomier abode.

- Add a mirror – it reflects light as well as the image of the room, giving the illusion of more depth.

- Declutter the room and make it tidier (see page 24 for how to do this).

- If your room is full of small items that are hard to tidy, use storage boxes or caddies to keep them organized and out of sight.

- Open up the room by making sure you don't have furniture in front of walkways or doorways.

- Place large items of furniture against the wall (for instance, placing a table lengthways rather than having it stick out into the room). The more floor you can see, the bigger your room tends to look.

- Choose light, soft tones for your walls and furnishings. This makes your room feel open and airy.

- Allow as much natural light into the room as possible. Make sure your windows are clean and, for rooms other than the bedroom, choose a light material for your curtains.

- Choose a unified colour scheme for the room – especially a paler, more neutral one if creating space is your priority.

- Add in a piece of floor-to-ceiling furniture, such as a dresser or a bookcase. Anything that draws the eye upward emphasizes the height of the room and makes your ceilings seem higher.

- If you have shelves, leave some empty space around each item rather than cramming the shelf full. This gives your room an airier look.

- Small decorations or ornaments can make a room feel cluttered no matter how neat you make them. Avoid this by opting for a few larger items instead.

- Use stripes running the length of the room – perhaps on a rug – to elongate your space.

LIGHT THE WAY

The way that your home is lit can have a significant effect on its atmosphere and on how you respond to each room. You might think that daylight and your single ceiling bulb are the only options, but there are many ways you can tailor your lighting to your needs and make your home feel most like *you*.

There are three main kinds of light to consider. Bedrooms and living rooms tend to have multiple purposes, so it works well to have a combination of all three types.

- **General light** – this is the main source of light for your room, usually coming from a fixture in the middle of the ceiling.

- **Task light** – these are smaller, focused sources of light for specific jobs, such as desk lights, reading lights or lighting under kitchen cupboards.

- **Mood light** – these are the smaller sources of light you can add to a room to accent certain elements and create different atmospheres.

TOP TIPS ON LIGHTING

- Make sure you have the correct base level of light in your room. Multiply the length and the width of your room (in metres), then multiply the answer by 250 and you will find the approximate number of lumens needed to light your space (lumens are a measure of light output). (Most lightbulbs will state how many lumens they have on their packaging).

- If you're not sure where you want to put your mood lights, try walking round with a lamp and watching how the different placement affects the feel of the room.

- If your ceilings are high or if you have dark colours on your walls, you may need to add extra light sources to prevent the room feeling gloomy.

- If you want your general lighting to feel soft and inviting, consider installing a few wall sconces or floor lamps rather than having one main light. This breaks up the light and gives the room a softer glow.

- If your general light source is coming from more than one light, make sure they are spaced evenly to prevent some areas of the room being more shadowy than others.

- If versatility is a priority, choose lights that can be dimmed and brightened, which gives you more control of the light levels. This also helps us to feel more connected to the natural world (see page 34), as you are able to adapt your lighting to mimic the movements of the sun.

- Consider the colour temperature of the light. For a cosy feel, opt for bulbs with a warmer colour temperature. For task lights, or a space where you need to be alert, opt for brighter bulbs with a cooler colour temperature.

MAKE YOUR BEDROOM A SANCTUARY

The bedroom is the part of the house in which we spend the most time. However, even though we're asleep for most of that time, it's still an important room and considering the way you use it will have a positive impact on your life.

Sleep is just as important as diet and exercise in keeping us healthy. It's the process that helps the body to heal itself, regulate hormones, process information and consolidate memories. Good sleep also improves your immune system, focus, energy levels and mood. Most of us don't get enough of it and this has a detrimental effect on our well-being. Multiple studies around the world have concluded that the less you sleep, the more likely you are to suffer a heart attack. For people aged 45 and over, getting 6 hours rather than 7 or 8 hours of sleep increases your risk by up to 200 per cent.*

The good news is that there is plenty you can do to improve your sleep and it starts with the bedroom itself. Here are a few tips on how to turn your bedroom into a haven for first-rate slumber:

- Wash your bedding often – at least once a fortnight, but ideally once a week – and air out the room every day if you can so that the room stays feeling fresh and inviting.

- Keep your room tidy and free of clutter so that it's somewhere you can relax.

- Make sure the things in your bedroom are just the essentials and items that you love. This is especially important if your room is small, as this will help to keep it clean and clear.

- Aim for the ambient temperature to be between 16–18°C (60–64°F), as this is the optimum level to promote good sleep.

- Make your room as dark as possible when it comes time to sleep. Choose a material for your curtains or blinds that's thick enough to block out the light.

- Keep your to-do list away from the bedroom! That means keeping the laundry basket, the work laptop and any other reminders of day-time tasks somewhere else.

* Matthew Walker, *Why We Sleep* (2018), p.165

EMBRACE CHANGE

It's a wonderful thing to be able to decorate our homes. Not only is it a form of self-expression, but we can find a great sense of peace and happiness when the space we're in matches how we feel inside.

However, the arrangement you settle on now, next month or next year doesn't have to be what you stick with forever. In fact, perhaps it shouldn't be! The only constant in life is change, and that's something that we all have to embrace if we are hoping to live fully and happily in the moment.

So, pay attention to yourself. Notice when your tastes and interests change and notice yourself evolving with time. If you feel that the person you are no longer aligns with the home you live in, don't be afraid to make some changes. Your decor may have been right some time ago, but that doesn't mean it's still right now. Stay in tune with how you feel and let instinct guide the way.

When you're happy at home, it spills out into every other area of your life.

Bobby Berk

BRING THE
OUTSIDE IN

As human beings we are deeply connected to the natural world, but modern life often means that we are separated from it. However, you don't need to live in a forest to stay in touch with nature. This chapter offers ways for you to bring the outside inside and celebrate its gifts all year round.

The great outdoors and you

Many people believe that humans have an innate connection to the natural world and that, no matter our surroundings, we will always be drawn toward it in some way. This is called biophilia – a passion for things that are natural and alive. The term was first coined in 1978 by psychoanalyst Erich Fromm, and it was used again in the 1980s by biologist Edward O. Wilson, who proposed that humans had a desire to seek out nature and that doing so had a positive effect on our mental health.

The science backs this up. Studies have shown that spending a total of two hours a week in green spaces has a marked improvement on your health and well-being,* and that taking any time to connect with nature is beneficial for your mental health, and can reduce symptoms of anxiety and depression.** When we think about human history, this isn't surprising. We evolved in the natural world; our bodies are adapted to walk in green spaces, to run, swim and explore. We were made to live in harmony with nature – not separate from it.

Bringing the outside indoors and incorporating it into our homes is a way to nurture the part of ourselves that is always

seeking a connection with nature. For instance, you can choose organic materials for your furniture and decor, such as wood, stone, reeds or cork; use natural fabrics such as linen, cotton or wool rather than manmade equivalents; or you could create your very own decorations from the treasures you find outdoors (read on for some inspiration).

However you choose to invite the outside world into your home, by doing so you are helping yourself to remain grounded in your environment and connected to nature.

* www.nature.com
** www.mind.org.uk

CREATE A SEASONAL DISPLAY

Having an area of your home where you can celebrate the seasons is a wonderful way to connect with the natural world and helps you to experience the changing seasons more fully. This area could be a small table, a window ledge or a mantlepiece where you display a few natural objects throughout the year. Refresh it as the seasons pass and enjoy engaging with the world around you, even from indoors. Here are some ideas about what could be included in your seasonal displays:

SPRING

- Spring flowers in a twig vase (see page 52)
- Art made from pressed flowers or leaves (see page 42)
- Pastel pinks, yellows, greens and blues
- A collection of leaf-painted eggs (see page 46)
- Feathers, petals or snail shells

SUMMER

- A summer wreath (see page 50)
- Bright, bold yellows, pinks and purples
- Sea-shell tealights (see page 53)
- A summer garland (see page 44)
- Sea glass and pebbles

AUTUMN

- A pinecone garland (see page 44)
- Oranges, browns and greens
- Acorn tealights (see page 53)
- Confetti from autumn leaves (see page 45)
- Pinecones, conkers, acorns, leaves

WINTER

- A pomander (created by studding an orange with cloves)
- A winter wreath (see page 50)
- Whites, reds, greens and browns
- Fir sprigs, winter berries and twigs
- A twig vase to display winter foliage (see page 52)

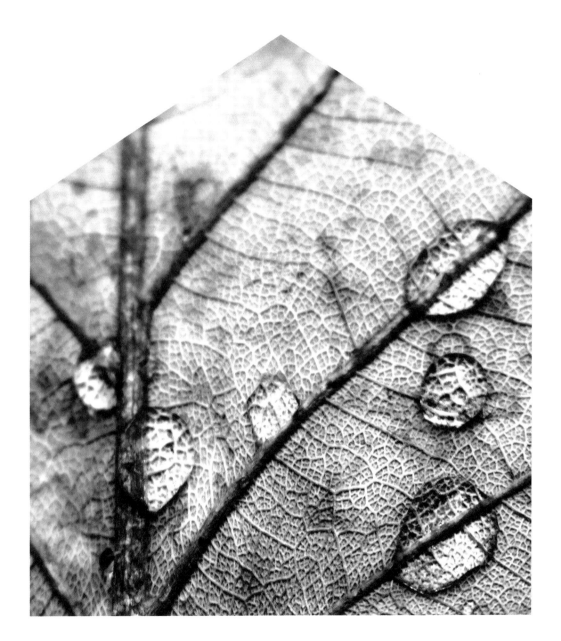

DRIFTWOOD HANGER

Adding driftwood to your home is a beautiful and functional way to bring the outside in, and the natural tones of the wood have a calming, grounding effect on a room. The bigger the piece of wood, the more you will be able to hang on your hanger.

Method

Ensure that your piece of wood is clean and completely dry. Sand down any rough edges to remove splinters.

Next, paint your driftwood, if desired, and leave until it is completely dry.

Find the side of the wood that lies the flattest (this will become the side that sits against the wall), then attach your picture hangers to this side using the screwdriver. Most small pieces of driftwood will be fine with one hanger on either end, but bigger pieces may need a third in the middle as well.

Hold the wood up against the wall and make a small pencil mark where each hanger is: this is where each picture hook will need to go. Use a spirit level to ensure the line is straight. Double check that your measurements line up with the hangers in the wood, then secure the picture hooks to the wall.

Finally, attach the screw-in hooks where you would like them to be on the front of the wood, using pliers if necessary.

Hang your creation on the wall and admire your handiwork.

You will need

Length of driftwood or fallen branch

Acrylic paint (optional)

Paintbrushes (optional)

Picture hangers and hooks (ensure these are strong enough to carry the weight of the things you will be hanging up)

Screw-in or "S" hooks

Hammer

Pliers

Screwdriver

PRESSED-FLOWER WALL ART

A dried flower can be used in many ways – in a journal or scrapbook, as a decoration to display in your home or as an addition to candles or soaps, to name but a few. This step-by-step guide shows you how to make a simple piece of art to hang on your wall so that you can be reminded of the outdoors every time you look at it. Although these instructions use only one flower, your design is completely up to you – be minimal or fill the frame with colours and shapes that bring you happy feelings and memories.

Method

Choose a flower to press. Make sure that the plant is healthy and not wilted or damaged. Remove any dirt from the stem (but keep petals dry), then trim the stem so the flower will fit inside your frame.

Choose a book that is the same length or longer than your flower. Cut two pieces of newspaper the same size as the book. Arrange the flower on one piece of newspaper, place it inside the book, then place the other piece of newspaper on top and shut the book gently.

Stack more books on top of the flower book so that the flower is being pressed by an even weight and leave it to dry for 3–4 weeks.

Once this time has passed, open the book and remove the flower from the newspaper. Be careful: the petals can be incredibly thin and delicate.

Gently apply PVA glue to the back of your flower with a paintbrush and place it on the white card.

Wait a few minutes for the glue to dry before placing the card in the frame. Then, hang up your creation and admire it!

You will need

Selection of flowers (or leaves)

Several heavy books

2 sheets of newspaper

Picture frame

PVA glue

Paintbrush

White card that fits into your frame

43

PINE CONE GARLAND

This simple garland adds character to any autumnal display. Once you're confident in your technique, why not try creating a garland with other natural materials, such as leaves, dried flowers or dried fruit?

You will need

Twine

Scissors

30–40 pine cones

Method

Cut 30–40 pieces of twine, approximately 25 cm (10 inches). Then take a pine cone and one piece of twine. Tie the twine around the bottom row of the pine cone's scales. Repeat for each pine cone.

Measure out another 90 cm (3 feet) of twine. Tie each end into a loop so you can hang your garland when it's done.

Then, take each pine cone and tie it to the larger piece of twine. When you're done, trim any loose ends of twine and hang your garland.

LEAF CONFETTI

You can use leaf confetti in scrapbooks or as decoration on a nature display – or you can throw it in the air for dramatic, celebratory effect! Here's how to make some of your own.

You will need

Fresh leaves

Craft punch (or punches)

Several heavy books

2 sheets of newspaper

Method

Take one of your leaves and put it inside the craft punch. Punch out a shape and place it on a piece of newspaper. Keep going until you have as many pieces of confetti as you'd like, making sure they don't overlap each other. Then place your second piece of newspaper on top, stack heavy books on top of them and leave the confetti to dry for 3–4 weeks.

You can experiment with mixing different leaf colours and different shapes for new effects.

HERB-PRINTED EGGS

As a symbol of new life and rebirth, eggs are a symbol that reminds us of all the new possibilities that spring brings. Whether you celebrate Easter or you just want some colourful springtime decor on your seasonal display, these naturally dyed eggs are the perfect fit. Archaeologists have found decorated eggs that date back 60,000 years, so by doing this craft you are also taking part in a tradition that's thousands of years old.

Method

First, roughly chop the cabbage, transfer to a large saucepan and add enough water to cover it. Slowly bring it to the boil, then put a lid on the pan and simmer it for an hour, or until the water is a deep-purple colour.

Meanwhile, lightly grease a plate with butter. Take a leaf, press it against the greased plate and then press the greased leaf on to the shells of the eggs. Add as many as you want in whatever pattern you'd like. Next, if you are using cheesecloth, wrap the egg in the fabric and secure it with twine or a rubber band. If you are using tights, cut off each foot, place the egg in the toes and secure with twine or a rubber band. Wrap the eggs tightly so that the leaves are held in place.

Strain the cabbage water into a bowl and add the vinegar. Stir briefly to combine, then submerge the wrapped eggs. Leave them there for at least two hours, or overnight if you would like them to have a stronger colour.

When the eggs have reached your desired colour, take them out of the water and leave them to dry in their wrappings on a clean towel. Once they are completely dry, remove the cheesecloth/tights and the leaves, and display.

You will need

1 red cabbage

3 tbsp white vinegar

4 large eggs, hard-boiled

Bunch of soft, delicate leaves, such as parsley or coriander

1 tbsp butter (or non-dairy alternative)

4 pieces of cheesecloth large enough to hold an egg, or two pairs of old tights you no longer use

Twine or rubber band

Natural dyes

Many common household foods and spices can be used as natural dyes. Why not try dyeing your eggs with:

- Beetroot (pink)

- Spinach (green)

- Carrots (pale yellow)

- Turmeric (strong yellow)

- Blueberries (blue)

- Coffee (pale brown)

- Onion skins (deep brown)

THE ENKINDLED SPRING

This spring as it comes bursts
up in bonfires green,

Wild puffing of emerald trees,
and flame-filled bushes,

Thorn-blossom lifting in wreaths
of smoke between

Where the wood fumes up and the
watery, flickering rushes.

I am amazed at this spring, this conflagration

Of green fires lit on the soil
of the earth, this blaze

Of growing, and sparks that
puff in wild gyration,

Faces of people streaming across my gaze.

And I, what fountain of fire am I among

This leaping combustion of
spring? My spirit is tossed

About like a shadow buffeted in the throng

Of flames, a shadow that's
gone astray, and is lost.

D. H. Lawrence

Nature always wears the
colours of the spirit.

Ralph Waldo Emerson

EVERGREEN WREATH

A wreath is usually associated with winter festivities, but they make a beautiful tribute to the seasons all year round. Here is a step-by-step guide to make a summer decoration.

Method

First, lay out all your greenery, grouping it by type. Then take smaller boughs and secure them together in a bunch using florist wire.

Attach the bunches to the wire frame one at a time with another piece of florist wire. Wind the wire around the stems and the frame a few times to secure it.

Work in one direction as you add more bunches to your frame, and make sure that bunches of greenery overlap so that the overall effect is thick and full, and there aren't any gaps.

When you've finished, check for any thinner parts or areas that are too bulky and make adjustments as needed. You could add in extra natural items, such as dried flowers, berries, or sprigs of leaves.

If you want to hang your handiwork, create a loop out of florist wire and attach it to the frame at the back of the wreath.

You will need

Metal wire wreath frame

Florist wire, cut into 13-cm (5-inch) strips

Wire cutters

Selection of 2–3 types of greenery (boughs of pine, spruce, holly, mistletoe, cedar, magnolia, ivy or boxwood work well)

Twine

TWIG VASE

This simple craft is an easy way to add rustic, seasonal charm to your table.

Method

First, cut the sticks to size using the handsaw.* The sticks should be approximately 2.5 cm (1 inch) taller than the height of your jar.

Next, use a glue gun to attach the sticks to the outside of your jar. Fill in any gaps with smaller, more flexible twigs. Depending on the look you would like, you could mix up varieties, textures and heights of twig.

Allow the glue to dry before using your vase.

You will need

Collection of sticks and twigs
   (the straighter the better)

Handsaw

Clean, empty jam jar

Glue gun

* When using a handsaw, make sure you follow safety guidelines and always wear eye protection.

SEASHELL TEALIGHTS

Forage for shells and bring calm beach-front vibes to your home with these simple but elegant tealights.

Method

Using a glue gun, secure one candle wick to the bottom of each shell.

Put the wax in a heatproof bowl, then put the bowl over a pan of simmering water.

Once melted, carefully pour the wax into each shell or use a teaspoon. Then leave the wax to cool. Make sure your shell is upright so the wax doesn't leak out.

Finally, cut off any excess wick and enjoy your seashell tealight.

You will need

Cockle shells,* washed and dried.

Glue gun

Candle wicks

Beeswax (or any other candle wax)

If you enjoy this craft, why not try making tealights in acorn cups for the autumn?

* When foraging, don't take too much from one area and make sure you don't take live cockles from the beach. Only collect the ones that aren't alive (their shells will be wide open), or single cockle shells that have detached from their other half.

AUTUMN

I love the fitfull gusts that shakes
The casement all the day
And from the mossy elm tree takes
The faded leaf away
Twirling it by the window-pane
With thousand others down the lane

I love to see the shaking twig
Dance till the shut of eve
The sparrow on the cottage rig
Whose chirp would make believe
That spring was just now flirting by
In summer's lap with flowers to lie
I love to see the cottage smoke
Curl upwards through the naked trees
The pigeons nestled round the coat
On dull November days like these
The cock upon the dung-hill crowing
The mill sails on the heath a-going

The feather from the raven's breast
Falls on the stubble lea
The acorns near the old crow's nest
Fall pattering down the tree
The grunting pigs that wait for all
Scramble and hurry where they fall.

John Clare

INDOOR GARDENING

You don't have to have a garden to be green-fingered. Whatever the space you're working with, there is always room for nature. And, as well as to giving you the rewarding experience of gardening and adding natural beauty to your home, having plants around you can improve your mood, increase your sense of positivity, fight stress and even increase your pain tolerance. There is also evidence to show that plants can purify the air in your house.* Whether you want a touch of greenery or an urban jungle, this chapter will guide you, with tips to help you choose, care for and style your plants.

* https://hside.org/plants-improve-mental-physical-health

HOW TO FIND THE PERFECT PLANT

From tiny succulents to giant cheese plants, and from upright aloe vera to tumbling ivy, there is a wealth of houseplants to choose from to suit every personality, every home and every level of expertise. Before you dive in to selecting yours, here are some things to consider:

LIGHT LEVELS

Does your home get a lot of natural light or is it shady? Sunnier spots will suit plants such as cacti or aloe vera, which come from hot, bright climates. Shadier homes will suit plants like philodendrons and snake plants, whose natural habitats are more sheltered.

SPACE

Before committing to a plant, check how big it is likely to grow. This is especially important if you have a small space! Even though they often start small, some house plants can grow to a metre or more in width or height.

HUMIDITY

Many plants thrive in a humid environment (for instance: ferns, ZZ plants and radiator plants), but others will not. Plants with thicker leaves, such as succulents, do better with drier air.

PET FRIENDLINESS

If you have pets, check that your chosen houseplant is safe for them; common favourites such as snake plants, pothos, peace lilies and philodendrons can all be poisonous to animals.

THE WONDERFUL
WORLD OF HOUSEPLANTS

Whether you want
something dainty or giant,
easy or more challenging,
there are houseplants to
suit every person, style,
home and budget.
Here are some ideas!

CHINESE
MONEY PLANT

Small-to-medium size

**Can grow in most light
conditions, but likes bright,
indirect sun. Pet-friendly**

**Prefers a medium
level of humidity**

PEACE LILY

Medium size

**Likes a combination
of light and shade**

Toxic to pets

Loves humidity

PHILODENDRON

Small-to-medium size

Prefers bright indirect sun

Toxic to pets

**Likes medium-to-
high humidity**

SPIDER PLANT

Medium size

**Can grow in most
light conditions**

**Not toxic, but can cause
harm to pets if ingested,
Likes some humidity**

SNAKE PLANT

Medium size

Needs low, indirect sunlight

Toxic to pets

Thrives in most
humidity levels

RUBBER PLANT

Medium-to-large size

Likes bright,
indirect sunlight

Toxic to pets

Prefers a medium-to-
high humidity

SUCCULENTS

Small size

Prefers bright light

Pet-friendliness varies
from plant to plant

Likes low humidity

CHEESE PLANT

Medium-to-large size

Likes rooms with
plenty of shade

Pet-friendly

Prefers a medium-to-high
level of humidity

ZZ PLANT

Small-to-medium size

Prefers bright light

Toxic to pets

Likes medium humidity

BOSTON FERN

Small-to-medium size

Prefers a shady spot
in a sunny room

Pet-friendly

Likes high humidity

Houseplants – the basics

When it comes to ideal conditions, each plant will have its own needs and preferences – much like us! When you buy your plant, all the key information about making it feel at home in your space will usually be included. However, here are a few tips to help you know what to look out for when caring for your green-leafed friends.

CHOOSE THE RIGHT SOIL

A soil mix that contains limestone is often a good choice as this extra ingredient balances out the acidity of the soil. If you have a cactus or succulent, choose soil with high water retention (look out for peat moss or perlite on the ingredients list). If you have a top-heavy plant, mix sand into the soil to give it a solid base and help to drain away excess water.

WATERING YOUR PLANT

Before you water your plant, push one finger down into the soil. In general, if the soil is dry 5 cm (2 inches) below the surface, it's time to water it. Make a note of your plant's watering needs when you purchase it, if possible, or look it up online to double check.

CLEANING YOUR PLANT

When a plant becomes dusty it can't photosynthesize as well, which interrupts its nourishment. To clean it, take a warm, damp cloth and rub its leaves in circular motions, taking extra care if your plant has delicate leaves.

WILTING LEAVES

If your plant has drooping leaves, this is usually a sign that it's not getting enough water. If watering the plant more often doesn't improve it, place some ice cubes on the surface of the soil – these will melt and provide gradual moisture through the day (although don't let the ice touch the plant).

Extract from

HORTULUS

Though a life of retreat
offers various joys,

None, I think, will compare
with the time one employs

In the study of herbs,
or in striving to gain

Some practical knowledge
of nature's domain.

Get a garden! What kind
you may get matters not.

Walafrid Strabo

Nature never hurries,
yet everything is
accomplished.

Lao Tzu

CREATE YOUR OWN TERRARIUM

A terrarium is a miniature greenhouse you can cultivate in the comfort of your own home. Not only are they a great way to connect with nature and enjoy the fun of gardening in an urban setting, but terrariums actually make it easier to grow some varieties of plants that like a high level of humidity – and they're great for small spaces. What's more, they're stylish and beautiful too! You can buy all the items to make your own terrarium online or from garden centres.

Method

Using a spoon, fill the bottom of the terrarium with a layer of soil. The amount of soil you need will vary depending on the size of your terrarium, but it should be deep enough to conceal the roots of your plants.

Place any decorative rocks or pebbles you would like to include inside the terrarium.

Make an indent in the soil large enough for each plant's roots. Then remove each plant from its container and place it in the garden using long tweezers or chopsticks.

Once you're happy with the position of each plant, spoon another thin layer of soil around the plants and pat it down firmly. The roots should all be covered.

Add any finishing touches – such as more pebbles or moss – then sit back and enjoy your mini garden.

You will need

Glass terrarium

Spoon

Soil

Decorative rocks or pebbles (optional)

Moss (optional)

Selection of plants (see notes below)

Long tweezers or chopsticks

The best plants for terrariums are small and slow-growing, such as succulents, radiator plants, Venus flytraps, sundew plants, dwarf palms, mini spider plants, maidenhair ferns or button ferns.

To care for your mini garden, put it in direct or indirect light as your plants require. It won't need watering often – perhaps every 3–6 weeks. Check the soil by poking into it with a finger; if your finger comes out dry, water the plants a little. Remove any yellow or brown leaves from plants when you see them. If you care for your terrarium well, it could be with you for many years!

COCONUT HANGING PLANT HOLDER

Here's how to make a simple coconut hanging plant holder so you can show off your plant family in style.

Method

First, paint your coconut shell with your chosen design and leave to dry.

Using your drill,* make five small holes in the coconut, four evenly spaced holes around the top (about 0.5 cm ($^1/_5$ inch) below the rim of the coconut) and one in the bottom for drainage.

Thread one piece of the string through each of the top holes. Tie a knot on the inner side of the coconut so that the string is secure.

Then add your soil and plants to the coconut shell.

Gather the tops of the string, tie them to the hoop and hang the plant from a ceiling hook. Philodendrons, Chinese money plants and small spider plants will work well in this planter.

You will need

Half a coconut shell

Acrylic paints

Hand drill

3 m (10 ft) length of string, cut into four

A keyring hoop

* Always wear eye protection when using a drill.

NO-NAILS HANGING PLANTS

If you can't drill holes or add hooks to your property, a repurposed clothing rail is a fantastic way to bring nature into your home, as it allows you to display a whole jungle of plants – without losing your deposit! It's also easy to move around, so not only does it create an elegant impromptu partition to any room, but it allows you to reimagine your space whenever you please.

Method

If desired, use your spray paint to change the colour of your clothing rail. Be sure to spray in a well-ventilated area (ideally outside).

Once the spray paint is completely dry, fasten your macramé planters to the clothes rail using the rope. Hanging your planters at different heights will create a more stylish display.

Place your plants into the macramé hangers and enjoy!

No space for a clothes rack? Hanging a plant or two on to the end of your shower rail is another great hack for renters.

You will need

A basic clothing rail

Macramé plant holders
  (see page 70 to make your own)

Rope for fastening

Spray paint (optional)

MACRAMÉ PLANT HOLDER

This classic planter design is simple to create, but gives you stunning results, and is best suited for planters of between 13 and 18 cm (5 and 7 inches) in diameter.

Method

Cut three pieces of rope so that they measure 1.4 m (55 inches) each.

Fold all three pieces of rope in half. Take the mid-point of the rope (the "loop") and pull it a little way through the ring. Then take the loose ends of rope and pull them through the loop. Tighten the knot against the ring.

Starting 20 cm (8 inches) down from the ring, take two loose ends, tie a half knot and then tie another half knot in the opposite direction. Pull from each side to secure the knot. Repeat twice more with the four remaining loose ends.

Measure 8 cm (3 inches) down from your row of knots and tie another series of three.

Then measure 10 cm (4 inches) down from your second series of knots, gather all six ropes together and tie into one large knot.

Trim the rope and hang from ceiling hook.

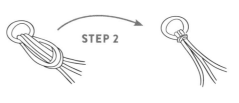

You will need

Scissors

Long cotton rope

A 5-cm (2-inch) wooden ring

STEP 2

STEP 3

WINDOWSILL HERB GARDEN

It's not just houseplants that allow you to experience gardening indoors – windowsill herb gardens are like having a tiny kitchen garden at your fingertips. Fresh herbs make your dishes come to life and, what's more, growing them yourself is economical and ensures your produce is organic and pesticide-free. It also reduces your carbon footprint in terms of the amount of food you purchase and the subsequent food waste you create. Here's how to make your very own windowsill garden.

Method

Clean your jam jars with washing-up liquid and warm water, then rinse and leave to dry. Fill the base of your jars with gravel, grit or small stones – make sure it's a minimum of 5 cm (2 inches) in depth. These stones are vital as they will draw the water and prevent mould forming on your plants.

Fill the jars about two-thirds full with compost. Plant three herb seeds in each jar (as a guide, plant the seed at a depth that's double the seed's thickness) and make sure the compost stays moist but not wet.

Once shoots start to form, add soil around the base of each plant and place on a windowsill – although if your chosen herb doesn't thrive in direct sunlight, find a shadier spot. Water them whenever the soil feels dry to the touch.

Now you can enjoy herbs all year round and they're easy to grab when you're preparing meals.

You will need

Herb seeds, such as parsley, thyme, basil, oregano, coriander, rosemary, mint or chives (you can purchase these from supermarkets or garden centres)

Selection of jam jars

Gravel, grit or small stones

Compost

Soil

I've yet to find a design conundrum that can't be solved with plants.

Justina Blakeney

Extract from

TINTERN ABBEY

... Therefore am I still
A lover of the meadows and the woods
And mountains; and of all that we behold
From this green earth; of all the mighty world
Of eye, and ear, — both what they half create,
And what perceive; well pleased to recognise
In nature and the language of the sense
The anchor of my purest thoughts, the nurse,
The guide, the guardian of my heart, and soul
Of all my moral being.

William Wordsworth

WORKING FROM HOME

The pandemic changed everyday life dramatically
and quickly; almost overnight, many people found
that their homes also became their workplaces.
Although there are many benefits to working
from home – such as no commute and more time
to spend with loved ones – these can quickly
be superseded by the disadvantages if our
workspaces aren't set up with our physical and
mental health in mind. This chapter will provide
you with plenty of tips to help you make any desk
environment in your home a calm and healthy one.

THE PERFECT DESK

For most of us, the most important piece of furniture for work will be your desk. You might say that it's just a table – but the way it's set up and the way you interact with it can have a significant effect on your well-being, so it's important to consider it carefully.

LOTS OF LIGHT

Make sure your desk is somewhere that gets plenty of daylight. Not only does this help you to see your work, but natural light promotes the release of the hormones such as serotonin and dopamine (also known as the "happy hormone"), boosts your mood and reduces anxiety. If you can't place your desk next to a window, there are other ways to make the most of your daylight: make sure your curtains or blinds are open as far as they can be and that your windows are clean. You could also use a mirror to bounce light around the room. If you work in a room with no windows, you could invest in a lamp that simulates daylight.

DECLUTTER

They say a tidy desk equals a tidy mind – and it's true! The tidier your surroundings are, the calmer your mind usually is as a result. Make sure everything you need is both organized and within easy reach, and that you don't have anything on your desk that you don't use.

NO NOISE

If you can, make sure your desk is somewhere where you won't be disturbed by noise. It's distracting, and extended periods in loud environments can trigger the brain's "fight or flight" response, which floods your body with cortisol, the stress hormone. If you don't have a quiet place to work, consider using earplugs or noise-cancelling headphones to help block out the world around you.

YOUR CHAIR

Even if you have the perfect desk, in the perfect place, it won't serve you unless you have the right kind of chair for your needs. When sitting at your desk, your eyes should be level with the top of your screen, your forearms should be able to rest comfortably on the desk and you should be able to put your feet flat on the floor with your knees at a 90-degree angle. An ideal chair will also support your back and help you to sit up straight.

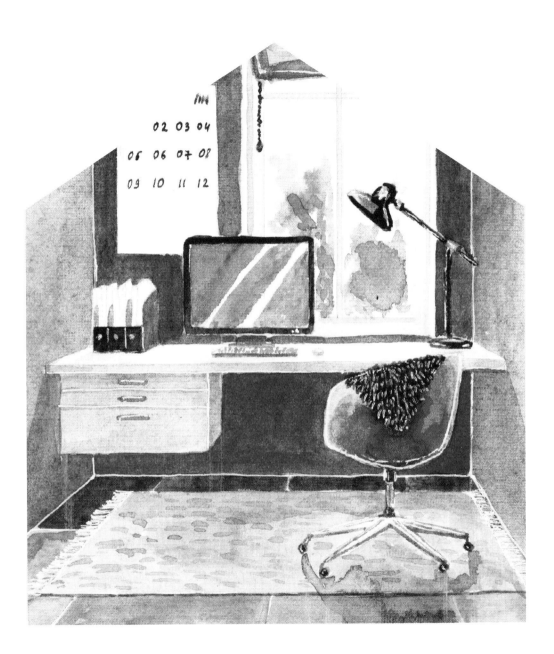

Looking after your body

When we're working from home, not only should we be mindful about our environment, but we must do our best for our bodies as well.

MOVE

Working from home often means that you're not moving as much as you would if you were going into your office or workplace, so it's important that you make time to move your body at regular intervals. Take a short walk around the house or garden every hour, and try to go outdoors in your lunchbreak and get some fresh air.

STRETCH

Performing regular stretches is another great way to look after your body as it helps to reduce fatigue, improve posture and circulation, and reduce feelings of tension.

• Here's a simple stretch to help counteract the effect of sitting over a screen: stand up with your feet hip-width apart and look straight ahead. Clasp your hands behind you and then lift them as high as you can.

- To stretch your hamstrings, first stand with your feet hip-width apart. Then, bend forward from the hips as far as you can go, keeping your neck and shoulders relaxed. Place your hands around the backs of your legs and hold the stretch for 30 seconds. Bend your knees, hold your stomach in and roll up slowly.

CONNECT

Many people find that working from home makes them feel isolated. To ensure that you stay connected to the world around you, reach out to others and stay in touch. Whether you have a ten-minute catch-up with a colleague or you talk to a friend, having moments of social connection can do wonders to boost your mood and keep you feeling balanced and happy.

SUBSTITUTE

Our environment plays a huge part in our working lives, and taking ourselves out of the building, away from the people and out of the structure of a regular workday can have a negative effect on our well-being. If you notice yourself feeling unhappy while you're working from home, think about your favourite parts of working in an office – perhaps it's reading in the park in your lunchbreak, chatting to colleagues or looking forward to a good cup of coffee from your local coffee shop – and try to implement something at home to make up for it.

PROTECT YOUR TIME

It's one thing to manage your time when you're at work – when you have a train to catch, or more rigid rules about when you do and don't need to be working – but when you're at home, it's different. The boundary between "work" and "home" is blurred, making it easier to start early and finish late, to sit at your desk for hours with no breaks or to feel like you should be checking emails even when you're not working. Even if you feel like you're getting lots done, this work ethic can take a toll on your mental health, so it's unlikely that you'll be producing your best results. There are plenty of things you can try to help reinforce the boundaries between time at work and time at home, even if you're in the same building (maybe even the same room).

- Make a schedule and stick to it. If you would normally start your workday at 9 a.m., make sure you're at your desk at that time, no sooner and no later. Set aside time for your lunch (away from your desk) and try your best to finish on time as well.

- If you live with other people, tell them your schedule. They might be able to help you keep to it, and this will let them know when you should and shouldn't be disturbed.

- Work at the time of day that suits you. If working from home allows you to be flexible with your schedule, make the most of this, and work when you know you're at your most alert and productive.

- Treat each day as if you were going into your workspace and dress appropriately. When you're at home, you may be tempted to wear pyjamas and slippers every day, but this doesn't do anything to help keep your work and home life separate – and, after all, when you dress the part, you feel the part!

- Don't mix housework with your work tasks. If you have a quiet moment, you might think of getting some chores out of the way (or a member of your household might request your help). However, if you're not certain you can do it in five minutes or less, don't do it. Stay in your work frame of mind, stay focused on your tasks and be firm about maintaining your work/home boundary.

TAKE A MOMENT TO PAUSE

Although there aren't many positives to a long commute, there is at least one: it's a natural pause between your workday and your time at home. However, when we work at home and we don't have this transition from one space to another, it's easy to rush straight from work into home activities, without stopping, which often introduces an unnecessary level of stress to your personal time.

When you finish your work day, try taking five minutes to pause and ground yourself in the present moment. Here are some ideas:

- Unfurl a yoga mat and lie on your back, allowing your body to completely relax. Close your eyes or keep them open – however you feel most comfortable. It may sound odd at first, but simply lying still can be incredibly calming.

- Do five minutes of yoga. If you are a beginner, there are plenty of tutorials online that can guide you through simple poses to refresh your mind, body and spirit.

- Light a candle and sit quietly in your space, breathing slowly and deeply, letting the glow of the candle soothe you.

- Dance! Helping your mind to calm down and change tack doesn't have to be done in stillness and quiet. Put on your favourite song and, for a few minutes, dance like nobody's watching and feel the pure joy of it!

A MINDFUL HOME

You've made your house feel like your home – but
are you connected to it? Our homes are not just
a base where we eat and sleep; they are a part of
us. They're where we begin and end our days, and
where we should feel most like ourselves. From
finding a space to truly call your own, to ideas for
daily mindfulness rituals, this chapter will help you
engage with yourself and your home, and help
you to carve out time and space for mindfulness.

A ROOM OF ONE'S OWN

A sacred space, a study, your room, a cosy nook – whatever you call it, having some form of private space that you can retreat to for some peace and quiet is vital for lasting well-being. It could be a whole room, or perhaps it could be a corner of another room that's arranged just for you. Whether you use this space as a study for work or as a place for creative pursuits, cultivating silence and a lack of interruption in this space will allow you to reach a deeper state of concentration. You might want to see it as an oasis in the midst of a busy life and use it as a place to relax, unwind and think.

You might go to it every day or only once in a while, but having this kind of space means that, however hectic your day, you always have somewhere that you can find some valuable solitude. If you only have a portion of one room to claim as your own and you live with other people, ask them to help you create this sense of solitude, by leaving you undisturbed whenever you are there.

Even if you're the kind of person who is energized by noise, stimuli and spending time around other people, it's still crucial for our mental health and overall happiness to be able to spend some time alone. Taking a few moments in quiet contemplation allows us to connect more fully to ourselves, and to take stock, whether that's in terms of our mindsets, our emotions, or of where we are in our lives and where we want to go.

CLEANSE YOUR SPACE

There are many reasons you might wish to cleanse your home – if you've had a bad day, if you've had an argument, if you've been ill, if you've recently experienced a big event or if you're generally feeling like there's a lot of negative energy in your space. Performing a cleansing ritual can help you break away from that energy and give you the feeling of starting afresh. This is especially important when it comes to your own room or private space, so that it remains inviting, and it continues to serve you and your well-being.

Provided you aren't sensitive to smoke, you could light a smudge stick, which is a bundle of dried herbs. Burning these bundles of dried plants and herbs is a practice that dates back thousands of years, and it's believed that doing so can help to cleanse your space and ward off any negative energy. Place your smudge stick inside a heat-proof container, or wear thick gloves, light the end and, when you see a flame, blow it out. You should then see embers at the end of the stick, which will emit a scented smoke. Take the smudge stick around your home, fanning the embers every now and then to encourage the smoke. You can buy smudge sticks ready-made or look up a tutorial online and make your own.

You could also use aromatherapy to reinvigorate your space and invite in new energy. The smell of citrus is uplifting and bright; to fill your home with this scent you could use lemon essential oil in a diffuser, or simmer sliced lemon or orange in a pot of water for a few minutes.

Set your intentions

Setting your intentions is a way to give yourself and your life direction and purpose. Here are some ideas about how you can use your home to help you make a bold and positive start, whether you're starting a new project or you want to ring in a new chapter, a resolution or even just a new day.

AFFIRMATIONS

Set up a morning affirmation routine. Pick a moment at the start of your day, whether it's first thing in the morning when you wake up, the moment before you get dressed or just before you leave the house. Take yourself somewhere meaningful in your home – the back garden, the mirror or your own private space. Once you're there, settle yourself and say your affirmation. For instance, "Today, I will take everything in my stride." This is an inspirational way to start the day, and having a routine to go with it will help to give it significance in your day.

INSPIRE YOURSELF

If you're starting a new project, have a tidy up before you begin. Clear your space of old papers or materials, and make sure your area is clean and uncluttered. You could then choose a picture, a quote, or an object that relates to your new challenge and reminds you of your goals, and put this somewhere prominent to inspire you while you work.

CRYSTALS

You can also charge crystals to help focus your intentions. For instance, charge a sodalite crystal for creativity or a citrine stone for prosperity. Refer back to the list of crystals on page 20 and choose one that suits your purpose. To charge a crystal, find a calm space, light a candle and spend a few minutes focusing on your intention. Then take your crystal and pass it over the candle flame three times. Keep the crystal in your space while you work on your project.

A MORNING RITUAL

Use your private space to help you practise a little self-care every day, by creating your very own morning ritual. The way your morning goes tends to set the mood for the day ahead, so by taking control of it and using it to consciously start well, you're setting yourself up for the day with a positive and calm frame of mind.

If you often find yourself rushing in the mornings, set your alarm a little earlier than usual to give yourself enough time.

When you wake up, take a moment to let your mind wander. Follow your thoughts and watch where they go. Then give them some more direction and focus on something positive.

Next, take yourself to your private space – or wherever it is in your home that you have carved out some room for you. Sit or stand quietly for a few seconds and then perform some stretches. A simple exercise is to straighten your spine (keeping your shoulders relaxed), raise your arms and reach for the sky. You could also try a few yoga poses or do a sun salutation. Finish by giving your arms a rub and hugging yourself. Then continue with your morning.

A morning ritual really can involve anything as long as it's something you can repeat and as long as it's something that makes you happy, whether it's a workout or simply standing outside in the fresh air for a few minutes. However you choose to do it, when you begin your morning with a few moments of mindfulness, you know you are ready to face the day and whatever it has to bring, as you will be starting from a place of calm.

If you want to conquer
the anxiety of life,
live in the moment,
live in the breath.

Amit Ray

Extract from

AUGURIES
OF INNOCENCE

To see a World in
a Grain of Sand

And a Heaven in
a Wild Flower

Hold Infinity in the
palm of your hand

And Eternity in an hour.

William Blake

AN EVENING RITUAL

When we spend a lot of our time at home, it's especially important to mark the transition points between different parts of our day. One point that's easy to neglect is the transition between the active part of your evening and the time when you are preparing for bed. Whether you've spent a hectic evening rushing around at home tackling your to-do list or you've been inundated with media input for an hour or two, try this ritual in your private space to help you unwind and begin to relax.

First, change into comfortable clothing, make yourself a hot drink if you like (herbal tea, or a different non-caffeinated drink), then take yourself to your room or a favourite space. You could light a candle for an extra calm ambience. When you are comfortable, take a piece of paper and note down the things that are on your mind – it could be specific worries you have or just a list of tasks that you need to complete the next day. Then fold up your paper and put it away in a drawer or somewhere else where it's out of sight.

If you still have time in your evening, choose something relaxing to do that will help you unwind. You could do some yoga stretches or guided meditation (there are apps that can help you with both of these things), or settle down with a book. Whatever you do, enjoy the feeling of disengaging with everything that happened during the day, and turning your attention to something that you're doing for the sake of relaxation and calm.

A COMMUNITY OF THE SPIRIT

Be empty of worrying
Think of who created thought
Why do you stay in prison
When the door is so wide open?
Move outside the tangle
of fear thinking
Live in silence
Flow down and down
Into always widening
Rings of being.

Rumi

With each breath we
have the opportunity to
begin again, to arrive in
the present moment.

Adriene Mishler

Embrace boredom

When you're living a busy life, one of the most valuable things you can do for your brain is to allow yourself to be bored. This is because when we're not bombarding ourselves with stimuli our brains are able to switch gear.

This gear is known as "default mode" – a kind of wakeful resting – and it's the human version of autopilot. In this mode, our mind is able to wander and daydream, and as it wanders it makes connections between past experiences and our present. This means that default mode helps us to come up with solutions to problems, to work through issues and to be creative. This mode also helps us to

take stock of our lives and get a bearing on our personal narrative, so it allows us to set goals and aspirations for the future too.

Make some time every week to practise being bored. Choose a space in your home and take a few minutes to sit quietly there – no phone, no music, no TV. You don't have to focus on your breathing or meditate. The aim is to do absolutely nothing at all. It might be uncomfortable to do at first, but it will become easier with practice. Allow your brain to be under-stimulated so that your mind can move freely and you can return to your day feeling restored.

A CALM SPACE

Even if you have a space of your own, it's easy for it to become associated with being busy or stressed, especially if you use that space to work on your own projects or ideas. Practising meditation, even for a few minutes a day, is a wonderful way to mitigate these feelings. Meditation has been scientifically proven to improve your focus and your mood, and help to reduce anxiety, stress and feelings of depression.* By meditating for a few minutes a day in your space, you can not only promote and maintain feelings of calm, but you can help to prevent your room from taking on negative or stressful associations, and ensure that it remains inviting.

There are many ways to meditate. Don't be afraid to try different methods to find out what works best for you. Here are three simple ideas to inspire you:

A BREATHING EXERCISE

Find a place where you can sit comfortably. Lightly place the tip of your tongue against the back of your front teeth. Keep it there throughout the exercise. Your mouth can be open or closed – however you feel most comfortable. Empty your lungs completely. Breathe in gently through your nose for 4 seconds. Hold the breath for 7 seconds. Exhale through your mouth for 8 seconds, allowing the breath to make a slight "whoosh" sound through your lips as you do so. Repeat this cycle another three times.

* www.headspace.com

A CANDLE MEDITATION

Bring a candle to a quiet, comfortable place. Turn off any bright lights, sit down and light the candle. Place it in front of you and focus on the flame. If any thoughts distract you, acknowledge them and refocus on the candle. Then, close your eyes, holding the image of the candle in your mind for as long as you can. Open your eyes to refresh the image if you need to. Practise this for a few minutes at a time.

PROGRESSIVE MUSCLE RELAXATION

Sit or lie somewhere quiet and comfortable. Relax your body; imagine all the tension seeping out of you. Let your breathing deepen and slow down. Then inhale slowly and contract one group of muscles. Hold them for a few seconds, then exhale as you release your muscles. Rest for 10 seconds, then move on to the next muscle group. You might like to start with your feet and work your way up your body. Take your time, and focus on the way that your body feels throughout.

If you don't have a fixed space that you can call completely your own, make a plan so that you can create this calm space when you need it. For instance, prepare a small bag or box containing everything you will need, such as a cushion, blanket or candle so you can easily take it to the place where you will meditate.

Meditation can help
us embrace our worries,
our fear, our anger; and
that is very healing.

Thich Nhất Hạnh

STAY CONNECTED

While it's important for all of us to spend time in solitude, we must also take care not to lose touch with the outside world. If you are spending the majority of your time at home, on your own or only interacting with a select few people, make sure to take the time to connect with others.

Many of us do this via social media, but although it's convenient, and a wonderful tool for sharing news and keeping in touch with distant friends, its ability to help us truly connect with one another is limited. Despite social media's aim being to bring people together, frequent use actually leaves us feeling more isolated than if we used it less.* Here are a few ideas to help you reach out to the ones you love, which will allow you to kindle that warm feeling of friendship and connection:

- **Write a letter or a postcard** – sitting down to put pen to paper will encourage you to compose a heartfelt message.

- **Phone or video call** – a typed message is never a true substitute for talking in real time, when you can hear the voice of your loved one (and even see them too!).

- **Create something with someone else in mind** – draw, paint, write, compose or craft. This is a thoughtful and unique way to show someone that you are thinking of them and that you care.

* www.health.harvard.edu/blog

A SUSTAINABLE HOME

Our planet needs our help and every little
thing we can do to reduce our carbon footprint
is a step in the right direction, because all small
actions add up. This chapter will show you
how to look out for the planet by decorating,
upcycling, getting creative and making
sustainable choices for your home life.

PLANET-FRIENDLY DECOR

When we are thinking about decorating our homes, our first instinct is often to look for something brand new. It's easy to assume that buying one piece of furniture won't add much to your carbon footprint – after all, many items are made from natural materials like wood or cotton, and if you use an eco-friendly mode of transport to collect your purchase from a shop, the impact on the planet seems minimal.

However, remember that with every manufactured product, there is an invisible cost to the Earth: the indirect carbon footprint. For instance, to create a wooden table, a vast amount of energy and water is needed to grow the trees and to manufacture the product, which will then usually be wrapped in plastic and shipped to a warehouse or a store. All this adds up to have a huge impact on the environment. It has been suggested that for every piece of furniture made, an average of 47 kg (104 lb) of carbon dioxide and its equivalents are emitted into the atmosphere, which is the equivalent of burning through 24 litres (5.3 gal) of petrol.*

The good news is there are plenty of ways to refresh your home space without buying new. From upcycling to repurposing and buying second hand, there are an abundance of ways to make planet-friendly choices when it comes to your decor, without having to sacrifice on style or budget.

Furthermore, not only is a sustainable lifestyle good for the planet, it's also beneficial beneficial for your health. It gives you a sense of purpose; this can improve your confidence as well as strengthening the connection between you and the natural world, which, in turn, promotes positive emotions, leaving you feeling lighter and happier. Living greener also helps you to be more mindful in day-to-day life and consider the impact of your choices.

* www.mytoolshed.co.uk

UPCYCLING

Upcycling is the art of taking a pre-loved item and giving it a makeover. With nothing but a bit of paint, some new fabric and some imagination, old, discarded or worn-out furniture can be given a whole new lease of life – and even sometimes a new identity! When you choose to upcycle rather than buy new, you are not only looking after the planet, but it usually saves you money as well. It's also an opportunity to get creative and express yourself and your style, as you have complete freedom to design as you wish.

Here are some upcycling ideas:

- Use bright fabrics to re-upholster chairs or sofas.

- Choose paints to give new life to desks, chairs or a set of shelves.

- Use discarded items in unusual ways. How about using a shutter as an organizer, a window or a vintage mirror as a message board, or an old ladder as a bookcase?

- Use stencils and paint to add interest to drawers or dressers. Don't worry if it goes wrong either – simply paint over your mistake and try again!

- Wooden pallets have the potential to be turned into many things, from bookshelves to tables to organizers. See page 116 to learn how to make a pallet coffee table.

- Add new doorknobs to doors, cupboards and drawers. Whether you choose colourful, eccentric, fancy or vintage designs, this is a way to refresh your space at very little cost.

- Old jars can be used as classy containers for small items.

- Many discarded objects can be used as creative planters. Bricks, shoes, old tyres, a watering can – pretty much anything that has space for soil has the potential to be a planter.

TOP TIPS FOR UPCYCLING

- Look around second-hand furniture stores, online auction sites, flea markets and car boot fairs for cheap items to upcycle.

- Make sure your items are clean and that they are structurally sound before you start (i.e. a lick of paint won't save a chair whose wood is rotting).

- A good paintbrush will give you a more professional finish and it will be less likely to leave bristles behind in your paint. To care for your brushes and rollers, wrap them tightly in oilcloth (secured with a rubber band) between coats and wash them as soon as you've finished the job.

- Consider waxing or varnishing your items when you're done. This helps to make your work last longer.

PALLET COFFEE TABLE

In their first lives, wooden pallets are usually used to store, protect and transport materials. You will often see them on building sites, in warehouses or being unloaded from vans and lorries laden with produce. Once their work is done, pallets are often discarded. However, this is when their second life begins. With the right tools, a simple wooden pallet can be upcycled into innumerable new things... including a coffee table. Here's how to make one of your very own.

Method

Begin by stacking your pallets to decide what looks best. Every pallet has its own unique characteristics, so this part of the process can take a little time.

When you have your configuration, prepare the pallets by fixing any areas that are loose or have split with wood glue and nails. Then use sandpaper to smooth the surfaces and prepare them for stain or wax polish.

Attach the pallets together with wood screws. If you're using any extra wood for the top of the table for a less rustic finish, cut it to size, lightly sand it down and attach it to the pallets with wood screws.

Apply the wood stain as per the instructions on the container.

Attach the castor wheels to the base of the table, one on each corner, making sure that they line up.

Your table is complete! For an extra-special finish, you can add a glass top, which can be cut to size by a picture framer or DIY store.

You will need

2 or 3 large packing pallets*

Extra wood planks for the top (optional)

Wood glue

Wood saw

Wood stain or wax polish

Nails and wood screws

Sandpaper

4 swivel-plate castor wheels

Glass for the top (optional)

* When you're procuring your pallets, be sure to ask before you take them away. You might want to consider getting hold of four or five pallets to give you more options in terms of size and finish.

NATURAL DYEING

Dyeing fabric with natural materials is an adventure and a beautiful way to celebrate the colours of natural world. It's also a cheap and fun way to breathe new life into the natural fabrics around you, such as cotton, wool or silk. So, if you're bored with your curtains, your cushion covers, your towels or your sheets, don't buy new ones – try dying them a new colour instead!

Almost anything can be used to create a natural dye, from onion skins and cabbage leaves to berries (and if you forage for your dye ingredients it makes your project even more special and memorable). You might be surprised at the results too – onion skins will yield a pink hue and a red cabbage will dye your fabrics an inky blue.

Method

Fill your bucket with cold water and place the item to be dyed in the water to soak for an hour.

Once the hour is up, fill an old saucepan or cooking pot with water and heat until it's on a rolling boil.

Add your mordant of choice. Ratios will vary but use 1 tsp of mordant per litre (1.75 pint) of water as a general guide. Stir until it dissolves.

Add the fabric and turn down the heat, place the lid on the pot and leave to simmer for 2 hours. Then remove from the heat and allow to cool.

Once cool, take out the fabric while wearing rubber gloves – just in case you are sensitive to the mordant. Rinse the fabric in cold running water and allow to dry on a washing line.

Now's the time to put on your apron! Next, create the dye by adding your plant material to the cleaned pot and enough water to cover the plants. Add your prepared fabric and slowly bring the water to the boil. Once boiled, cover and simmer for an hour, stirring occasionally with a wooden spoon and checking the colour every so often by lifting the fabric. Remember the shade will be significantly paler once the fabric has dried.

When you are happy with the colour, turn off the heat and allow the fabric to soak in the dye until cool.

Take out your fabric and rinse in cold running water. Allow to dry.

Wash your hand-dyed items separately when washing for the first time, just in case the dye hasn't set sufficiently.

You will need

Bucket

The item you want to dye

Large old saucepan or cooking pot with a lid (you won't want to use it for cooking after this!)

Mordant (this is fixative, necessary to hold the colours; alum is best and can be found in supermarkets as it's often used as a preservative, but if you want to go au naturel, lemon juice or white wine vinegar will do the job)

Rubber gloves

Apron

Your choice of non-poisonous plant for dyeing

Wooden spoon

STRIPED YARN LAMP

You can spend a lot of money on acquiring the perfect items to furnish you home – but you don't have to! This yarn-decorated lamp is one example of how you can take a basic item and spruce it up so that it's exactly what you want – and keep your carbon footprint to a minimum too.

Method

First, put a line of glue along the bottom of your lampshade.

Following the glue, start to wrap the yarn around the lampshade. Adjust it with your fingers so that the yarn sits flat against the edge. Continue wrapping and gluing, using your fingers to push the yarn down as needed so that it sits flush against the piece underneath.

When you have a coloured stripe on your lampshade of the desired thickness, cut yarn number one and glue the loose end in place. Then begin gluing and wrapping yarn number two.

Repeat this process until you have covered the whole lamp to your liking.

You could experiment with different colours, patterns and sizes of stripe.

You will need

Lampshade (a cylindrical fabric lampshade is best)

Yarn in desired colours

Glue gun

PATCHWORK STATEMENT WALL

A statement wall is a great way to establish your sense of style and your personality. By using offcuts and scraps of wallpaper, you can create bold, original displays of colour and pattern.

There are different ways to approach this particular craft. You can use similar patterns and colours, or mix ones that clash. You can place each piece of paper neatly so that the squares are aligned, or you can overlap them for a jazzier, more relaxed feel. Take a look at other patchwork walls online to be inspired. If you don't already have scraps of wallpaper, they can be found cheaply online.

Method

If desired, trim down your scraps so that each one is the same size. Use scissors or a box cutter for this (if you are using the latter, make sure that you have a protective piece of carboard beneath the paper). If your scraps are a wide variety of sizes, you might choose to have two uniform sizes that you trim them down to.

Then begin to lay out your design. Do this on the floor first so you can edit and experiment as you go. If you have pieces of different sizes, start with the bigger pieces first.

When you're happy with your design, start to secure it to your wall. Take one scrap and lightly spritz it with water (this is especially important if any of the paper you are using is old or brittle). Using a brush, spread a layer of wallpaper paste on the back of the scrap and place it in the desired position on the wall. Smooth it down with your hands so that there are no bubbles. Repeat for the remaining pieces of wallpaper until the whole wall is covered to your liking.

Wait for the wall to dry, then stand back and admire your handiwork!

You will need

Wallpaper squares (enough to cover your wall)

Scissors, or a box cutter and protective surface

Spray bottle of water

Wallpaper paste

Paintbrush

If you want to try this technique but don't want to commit to decorating a whole wall, why not try it on a cupboard or a chest of drawers instead?

SUSTAINABLE HOME SPA

Being good to the planet doesn't mean you can't pamper yourself from time to time. Here's how to create an eco-friendly spa experience from your very own home, all with natural ingredients.

EXFOLIATING FACE SCRUB

With clean fingers, mix 1 tbsp soft brown sugar with 1 tbsp honey, then apply to your face in small circular motions. Rinse with warm water.

MOISTURIZER

Mix ½ cup coconut oil with ½ tsp vitamin E oil and an essential oil of your choice. Mix thoroughly, then freeze for 5–10 minutes. Using a fork, stir the mixture until it has a smooth consistency and store in an airtight container. Apply as usual.

SOOTHING FACE MASK

Mash one medium banana until smooth, and mix with ¼ cup plain yoghurt and 2 tbsp honey. Apply to your face and neck and leave for 10–20 minutes. Rinse off with cold water.

FOOT SOAK

Fill a bowl or bath with 2 litres of warm water. Add 35 g baking soda and stir it in until it dissolves. Soak your feet for 30 minutes, then rinse them and pat dry. (Why not use the water in your garden when you're done?)

HEALTHY HAIR MASK

Mix 2 tbsp coconut oil, 4 tsp demerara (raw) sugar and 3 drops peppermint essential oil. Apply the mixture to clean, towel-dried hair that's still slightly damp. Massage it into your scalp, then leave it in for 10–20 minutes. Rinse with warm water.

WOODEN BATH CADDY

There's nothing better than relaxing in the bath with your favourite drink, a good book and a candle. Instead of balancing everything around the side of the bath, why not try this simple DIY project and make your very own reclaimed-wood bath caddy?

Method

Measure the width of your bath. Make sure you measure right to the edges (not just the inner part), as your board will need to be long enough to sit across the bath.

Using a handsaw, cut the length of wood to size. Then sand down the whole piece of wood until there are no sharp edges.

Apply wood stain to the board if desired and allow to dry completely.

Finally, apply wood wax, which will help to protect the wood from moisture.

You will need

Length of wood

Measuring tape

Handsaw

Sandpaper

Wood stain (if desired)

Wood wax

How to source your wood
You may be able to find wooden boards at a flea market or car boot sale, but if not, look online to see if there are any centres near you that offer reclaimed boards.

EAT GREEN

One of the biggest positive choices you can make toward helping the planet is to eat less meat. The meat itself is not the issue – it's all the energy that goes into producing it that has an impact on the planet. The process of rearing, keeping and transporting farm animals takes around 11 times more fossil fuels and six times more water than plant-based foods, which is why cutting down on your meat consumption is a good way to minimize your carbon footprint. Having a meat-free diet also contributes to a healthy lifestyle; people who don't eat meat tend to consume more portions of fruit and vegetables per day as well as less saturated fat. Here are a few tips on how to eat less meat and more plants:

- Don't pressure yourself to make changes too fast. If you currently eat meat every day, start slowly and try to have one meat-free day per week. If you have meat three times a week, try having it only once or twice a week. The key to making a lasting change is to go gradually.

- Explore vegetarian meat substitutes: vegetarian mince, fake meat, seitan or tofu.

- Find vegetarian alternatives for your favourite meaty dishes – Bolognese made with vegetarian mince; portobello mushrooms or cauliflower instead of steak; pulled pork-style jackfruit; bean burgers with coleslaw; or curries with aubergine instead of meat.

- Take the pressure off by planning your meals ahead of time. It makes meals one less thing to think about every day.

- Don't eat meat just for the sake of it – if you have a pasta bake or stir fry and always throw in chicken or bacon out of habit, try substituting meat for an extra vegetable.

- Eat plenty of beans. Not only are they an excellent way to consume the nutrients that you'd usually get from meat, but they are low in fat and often a meaty substitute in themselves.

- Add cereal and grains, such as couscous, quinoa, rice or barley to your meals and salads. They are high in protein, so help to make up the nutritional value from cutting out meat.

- If you're peckish, snack on nuts that are rich in protein and healthy fats. Almonds, pistachios and hazelnuts are all excellent options, and you only need a small handful to fill you up for hours.

- Have fun and be inspired: explore vegetarian cookbooks for more ideas. If you're used to meat featuring as the main part of your meal, this is a particularly good way to change your perspective and see that vegetables can also be the star of the show!

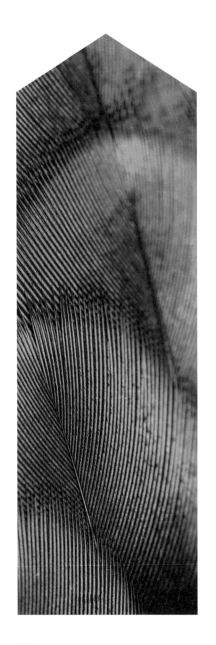

"HOPE" IS THE THING WITH FEATHERS

"Hope" is the thing with feathers –
That perches in the soul –
And sings the tune without the words –
And never stops – at all –

And sweetest – in the Gale – is heard –
And sore must be the storm –
That could abash the little Bird
That kept so many warm –

I've heard it in the chillest land –
And on the strangest Sea –
Yet – never – in Extremity,
It asked a crumb – of me.

Emily Dickinson

You are never
too small to make
a difference.

Greta Thunberg

THE HEART
OF THE HOME

The kitchen is the heart of any home, so fill
yours with warmth, light and joy by cooking
up some delicious dishes. Whether you like
the smell of baking bread, the inviting aroma
of a piping hot lasagne or fresh chocolate
chip cookies, this chapter has plenty of heart-
warming comfort food recipes to make
your home (and your stomach!) feel full.

TOMATO SOUP FOR THE SOUL

This soup is rich and comforting – truly a hug in food form. It goes well with a side of fresh crusty bread or served with a dollop of extra-creamy mashed potato.

SERVES 2

Method

Heat the oil in a saucepan over a medium heat. Add the onions, stir briefly and allow to cook for a couple of minutes.

Carefully crush the garlic cloves by pressing each one onto a chopping board with the flat of a large knife. Add the garlic to the pan, put the lid on, turn the heat to low, and leave the onions and garlic to sweat for 10 minutes. Stir them periodically so that they don't stick to the bottom of the pan.

Add the plum tomatoes to the pan and crush them gently with a spoon so that they are broken up. Then add the sugar and vegetable stock. Bring the contents of the pan to the boil then reduce the heat to a simmer and leave with the lid on for 30 minutes. Keep an eye on the water level. If it looks like it's getting low, add a little more.

Remove the pan from the heat, pour the contents into a blender and blend until completely smooth. Stir in the butter and add salt and pepper to taste. If desired, stir in a few spoonfuls of milk or cream to make your soup extra special.

Ingredients

1 tbsp oil

1 onion, chopped

4 cloves garlic, peeled

1 tin plum tomatoes

1 tsp dark brown sugar

350 ml (0.7 pt) vegetable stock

Knob of butter

Salt and pepper to taste

Milk or cream (optional)

HEARTY VEGGIE LASAGNE

There aren't many problems that a giant serving of lasagne can't fix. This recipe works best with the vegetables chopped as small as possible so that the flavours blend together in the sauce.

SERVES 2–3

Method

Preheat the oven to 180°C fan/350°F. Set your lasagne dish to one side (approx. 20x30 cm or 9x13 inches).

Heat the oil in a large frying pan and add the onion. Fry over a medium heat until the onions are translucent. Then add the garlic and fry for another minute.

Drain and rinse the lentils, then add them to the pan along with the carrot, mushrooms, tomatoes, wine, soy sauce, herbs, sugar and salt. Stir well until combined, then reduce the heat and simmer the mixture for 25 minutes, or until the sauce is thick.

Meanwhile, make the white sauce. Add the butter to a medium saucepan over a low heat and allow it to melt. Then add the flour and whisk until you have a thick paste. Take the pan off the heat and add the milk a few teaspoons at a time, whisking between each addition until the sauce is completely smooth. When all the milk has been added, return the pan to a medium heat and stir constantly until the sauce has thickened (usually a few minutes).

Construct the lasagne by layering ragu, pasta sheets and white sauce alternately, ending with a layer of white sauce. Sprinkle parmesan over the top, then bake for 40–45 minutes.

Ragu

1 tsp olive oil

1 onion, diced

3 cloves of garlic, minced

1 can green lentils

1 large carrot, diced

300 g (10 oz) mushrooms, diced

2 cans chopped tomatoes

200 ml (7 fl oz) red wine

2 tsp dark soy sauce

1 tsp oregano

1 tsp sugar

1 tsp salt

White sauce

40 g (1.4 oz) butter

5 tbsp flour

550 ml (1 pt) milk

Other

1 box lasagne sheets

Parmesan, grated

WARMING RED LENTIL DAL

This dal is as delicious as it is quick to make. It's perfect if you want a warm, cosy weeknight dinner.

SERVES 3

Method

Put the lentils in a pan and add cold water until the lentils are just covered, then bring to the boil. Use a spoon to remove any "foam" that rises to the top. Once the water boils clear, add half of the butter and allow to simmer for 5–10 minutes until the lentils are soft.

Meanwhile, heat the oil in a large frying pan, then add the onion. Fry over a medium heat until the onion is translucent, then add the garlic, tomatoes, coriander, chilli powder, ginger and the curry powder. Stir well to combine and fry for another 2 minutes.

Add the spinach and stir until it has wilted, then drain and add the cooked lentils. Add in the juice of half a lime and season to taste.

Serve with rice or naan.

Ingredients

250 g (9 oz) dried red lentils

40 g (1.4 oz) butter

1 tbsp vegetable oil

1 red onion, diced

3 cloves garlic, minced

1 tomato or a handful of cherry tomatoes, diced

1 tsp ground coriander

1 tsp chilli powder

1 tsp ginger

2 tsp curry powder

100 g (3.5 oz) spinach

Juice of half a lime

RUSTIC HERB BREAD

Bread-making is often described as meditative. It takes time, patience and care, and it can't be rushed. Enjoy this feeling yourself with this recipe for herb bread – the end product would go very well with a bowl of tomato soup from page 134.

MAKES ONE SMALL LOAF

Method

Add the flour, yeast, salt, herbs and parmesan to a bowl and stir together. Add the water and slowly mix the ingredients with a wooden spoon, or using clean hands if needed. The dough will be sticky at this stage.

Shape the dough into a ball in its bowl, then cover it and leave it to prove for 3 hours at room temperature. It should double in size.

Prepare a baking tray by dusting it with flour and set it to one side. Then turn the dough on to a clean, floured worktop and use your hands to encourage it into your desired loaf shape. Then allow the dough to rise, covered, for another hour.

Meanwhile, preheat the oven to 220°C fan/420°F. Score the top of the dough – three slashes works well for a long loaf, and a cross works well for a circle. Then bake for 20–25 minutes. If you tap the bottom of the loaf and it sounds hollow, it is done.

Allow the bread to cool for a few minutes before serving. It's best consumed as soon as possible, but can last for three to four days, loosely covered, in a cool, dark place.

Ingredients

230 g (8 oz) bread flour, plus extra for kneading

1 tsp instant yeast

1 tsp salt

2 tsp dried basil

1 tsp dried oregano

40 g (1.4 oz) parmesan, grated

4 cloves garlic, minced

180 ml (6 fl oz) water (cool to the touch, but not cold)

The way you feel
about food sits hand in
hand with the way you feel
about yourself, and if you eat
happily and wholeheartedly,
food will make you strong.

Ruby Tandoh

RECIPE FOR A SALAD

To make this condiment, your poet begs
The pounded yellow of two hard-boiled eggs;
Two boiled potatoes, passed through
kitchen sieve,
Smoothness and softness to the salad give.
Let onion atoms lurk within the bowl,
And, half suspected, animate the whole;
Of mordant mustard add a single spoon,
Distrust the condiment that bites so soon;
But deem it not, thou man of herbs, a fault
To add a double quantity of salt;
Four times the spoon with oil
from Lucca crown,
And twice with vinegar, procured from town;
And, lastly, o'er the flavoured compound toss
A magic soupçon of anchovy sauce.
O green and glorious! O herbaceous treat!
'T would tempt the dying anchorite to eat.

Sydney Smith

SPICED APPLE AND BLACKBERRY CRUMBLE

The crumble is surely the queen of comforting food. Both sweet and sharp, crunchy and soft, this recipe is a heavenly combination of all the things a dessert should be.

SERVES 8–10

Method

Preheat the oven to 180°C/350°F and grease a 20-cm (8-inch), round, ovenproof dish.

Peel, core and chop the apples into roughly 1-cm cubes. Then rinse the blackberries. Add the fruit to a large pan along with a tablespoon of water and a tablespoon of the sugar. Cook the fruit uncovered on a low heat for 5 minutes, stirring occasionally, until it has softened a little. Once done, add the rest of the sugar, the cinnamon, allspice and salt. Stir thoroughly to combine and put to one side.

Meanwhile, put all the topping ingredients into a bowl and rub them together with the tips of your fingers until they resemble breadcrumbs. Alternatively, add all the ingredients to a food processor and pulse to achieve the same effect.

Put the fruit mixture into the bottom of the prepared dish, then sprinkle the crumble topping over the fruit evenly.

Bake for 30–40 minutes, until the fruit is bubbling and the top is golden brown. Allow to cool on a cooling rack before serving.

Note: make this recipe vegan by using dairy-free butter.

For the topping

200 g (7 oz) plain flour

150 g (5 oz) brown sugar

160 g (5.6 oz) butter

½ tsp salt

For the filling

300 g (10 oz) cooking apples

160 g (5.6 oz) blackberries

60 g (2.1 oz) brown sugar

1 tbsp plain flour

2 tsp cinnamon

1 tsp allspice

½ tsp nutmeg

½ tsp salt

CHEWY CHOCOLATE CHIP COOKIES

If your dream cookie is somewhere between crunchy and chewy, and full of chocolatey chunks, then this is the recipe for you.

MAKES 20–24

Method

Preheat the oven to 170°C fan/340°F and line a tray with baking paper.

Add the butter and both sugars to a large bowl, and cream together with an electric mixer until the mixture is pale and fluffy. Add the egg and vanilla essence, and mix again until combined.

Add the salt, baking soda, baking powder and flour to the bowl, and mix again until the dough starts to come together in clumps. Then add in the chocolate and use a spoon to stir the mixture until everything is combined.

Using clean hands, roll the mixture into balls and set on the baking tray. Make sure you leave at least 5 cm (2 inches) between each one. (Don't worry if the balls don't all fit onto one baking tray. Simply cover them and keep them in the fridge while the first batch is baking, or prepare a second tray.)

Sprinkle a tiny pinch of salt over the dough balls so that each cookie will have a few grains on the top. Then bake for 10 minutes or until the edges start to go a golden brown. When you take them out of the oven, they will still be soft in the middle, so allow them to cool and firm up for 5–10 minutes before transferring them to a cooling rack.

Store in an airtight container and eat within one week.

Ingredients

115 g (4 oz) butter

50 g (2 oz) caster sugar

150 g (5 oz) brown sugar

1 egg

1 tsp vanilla essence

⅓ tsp salt, plus extra for sprinkling

½ tsp baking soda

¾ tsp baking powder

200 g (7 oz) plain flour

150 g (5 oz) chocolate, roughly chopped into small chunks

HOMEMADE STRAWBERRY JAM

Jam is another meditative culinary adventure. You could buy it from a shop, but then you'd miss out on the calming process of preparing the fruit, watching the rich colour of the jam develop and listening to the soft, thick bubbling of the hot sugar.

MAKES 3–4 JARS

Method

Put the strawberries and the sugar in a large bowl. Stir until they are well mixed and leave lightly covered overnight at room temperature.

On the following day, sterilize your jars and lids. Preheat the oven to 120°C fan/250°F. Meanwhile, wash the jars and lids in hot, soapy water and rinse. Then put them on a baking tray and leave them in the oven to dry out for around 10 minutes. If any of your jars have rubber seals, remove them before this stage and boil the rubber instead to sterilize.

Then uncover the strawberries and transfer the whole mixture to a large pan, along with the lemon juice, and cook on a low heat. When the sugar has completely dissolved, turn the heat up and bring it to a boil.

Boil the strawberries for 10 minutes or until the jam is 105°C/221°F C on a cooking thermometer. If you don't have a thermometer, spoon a small amount of jam on to a cold plate. Wait for 30 seconds, then push the jam gently with the tip of a spoon. If it wrinkles, the jam is hot enough. If not, leave it a little longer.

Spoon the jam into your jars. Add a wax disc (or baking paper disc) to the top of the jam and immediately put the lid on. Store in a cool, dry place for up to a year.

Ingredients

750 g (1.6 lb) strawberries, hulled and halved (or quartered, if they're big)

750 g (1.6 lb) jam sugar

1 tbsp lemon juice

Equipment

Jam jars, sterilized

Waxed discs or baking paper cut to the size of the jar

Cooking thermometer (optional)

Using frozen strawberries
First, thaw the strawberries. Instead of leaving them to sit in sugar overnight, tip them into your large pan and fry them over a low heat for 10 minutes. Then add your sugar and lemon juice, and continue to stir until all the sugar has dissolved. Then bring it to the boil and follow the rest of the recipe as normal.

HOW TO BE A HOME BARISTA

One of life's simplest pleasures is enjoying a leisurely cup of coffee in a café. However you choose to enjoy it – whether you like to sit outdoors and watch the world go by as you sip, or you prefer to huddle inside among the happy noise of crockery, chatter and the coffee machines – there's no reason you can't recreate this experience in your own home.

Here are some handy tips to help you make coffee like a bona fide barista. Whether you can't make it out to the shops, or you just prefer stay in the comfort of your own living room, you can get the perfect cup every time, just the way you like it:

HOW TO MAKE COFFEE SHOP FOAM

If you don't have a coffee machine with a steaming wand, you can create foam with either a hand-held whisk or a clean, empty jar. First, heat the milk until it's between 60–68°C (140–155°F). For the jar method, pour the milk into a jar, seal the lid and shake vigorously until thick froth forms. Hold the jar with a tea towel to prevent your fingers burning. For the whisk method, put the milk in a jug, take a whisk between your palms and rub your hands together, whipping the milk until you get foam. For thicker, stronger foam, shake/whisk the milk for longer, and before you pour it into your cup, tap the jar/jug and swirl it lightly to even out the foam.

CAPPUCCINO

Using a coffee machine, or the method mentioned above, steam/foam 120ml (4.1 fl oz) of milk. Set to one side. Pour 80 ml (2.7 fl oz) espresso into a wide, shallow coffee cup and stir in sugar if desired. Then add the milk, using a spoon to hold back the frothiest foam until the end.

MOCHA LATTE

Add 50 g (2 oz) grated chocolate to 160 ml (5.6 fl oz) milk in a saucepan and heat slowly. Stir constantly until the chocolate is melted and the milk is nearly boiling. Add this to 60 ml (2 fl oz) brewed coffee and serve.

ICED COFFEE

Pour 1 cup of brewed, chilled coffee into a blender with 2–3 tsp sugar, 50 ml (1.5 fl oz) of water and 5 ice cubes. Blitz until smooth and serve immediately in a chilled glass. (Add ingredients such as honey, cinnamon or cream for an extra special cup).

HOT TOFFEE COFFEE

Pour 1 tbsp toffee/caramel ice cream, 175 ml (5.9 fl oz) hot coffee and 1 tbsp chocolate sauce into a mug and stir until smooth. Reheat for a few seconds if the ice cream has cooled the mixture too much. Top with whipped cream and a sprinkling of toffee chunks.

Note: if you have a dairy-free diet, substitute the milk, toffee and chocolate elements in any of these recipes for the barista version of your favourite vegan milk.

One cannot think well,
love well, sleep well,
if one has not dined well.

Virginia Woolf

Extract from

TO AUTUMN

Season of mists and
mellow fruitfulness,

Close bosom-friend of
the maturing sun;

Conspiring with him how
to load and bless

With fruit the vines that
round the thatch-eaves run;

To bend with apples the
moss'd cottage-trees,

And fill all fruit with
ripeness to the core;

To swell the gourd, and
plump the hazel shells

With a sweet kernel

To set budding more.

John Keats

CELEBRATE INDOOR PICNICS

Picnics are a simple thing to be treasured. Whether you're on the beach, out in a grassy field, secluded in a forest or just in the local park, something about eating outdoors takes even the humblest food and makes it magical. But what about when the weather turns, when plans change or when you're not able to go outside? The good news is that with a little imagination, you can still enjoy a picnic atmosphere from the comfort of home – and there are sure to be fewer unwanted six-legged guests.

First, you need to set the scene. Here are some of the things you might need. At the most basic level you'll just need a blanket and somewhere to sit, but why not go all out and create a fairy-tale-like hideaway in your own living room?

- A blanket

- Cushions to sit on

- Plates, cutlery and glasses (camping versions, if you have them)

- A tent or indoor teepee

- Fairy lights

- Bunting

Next comes the most important part: the food! As you're at home you can afford to be more adventurous when it comes to your choices, as the kitchen is just a few steps away. Here are some ideas to help inspire you.

Spring picnic ideas: quiche tartlets, chicken and salad baguette, scotch eggs, vegetable crisps, potato salad, Victoria sponge cake, strawberry shortcake and cream.

Summer picnic ideas: falafel wraps, strawberry and avocado salad, carrot sticks and hummus, focaccia with Mediterranean vegetables, summer berries and cream, mini trifles.

Autumn picnic ideas: roasted vegetable salad, a cheeseboard including grapes, nuts, dried fruit, crackers and vegetable sticks, apple and blackberry flapjack, cinnamon buns.

Winter picnic ideas: soup or stew in a cup, pasties, savoury muffins, ciabatta rolls with warming fillings (such as spicy chickpeas and salad), s'mores toasted over a tealight.

Home is not a place.
It's a feeling.

Cecelia Ahern

Last word

With the help of the tips in this book, hopefully you will now feel inspired to make the most of your home and have a few ideas about where you'd like to start, whether that's by changing up the decor, experimenting in the kitchen, bringing the outside in, or making both mental and physical space for mindfulness.

The world we live in is fast-paced and busy, so we must be increasingly proactive about taking care of ourselves. By making sure your home is a source of joy and contentment, you are taking a huge step toward doing this. Even making just one tiny positive change to your environment can help you feel in control, and it goes a long way to ensuring that your home truly feels like your own space.

The most important thing is that you have somewhere to come back to at the end of the day where you can relax and be yourself. Home is safety, home is happiness and home is you – and there's no place quite like it.

HOME, SWEET HOME

'Mid pleasures and palaces
though we may roam,

Be it ever so humble, there's
no place like home;

A charm from the skies seems
to hallow us there,

Which seek through the world,
is ne'er met with elsewhere.

Home! Home! Sweet sweet home!

There's no place like home!
There's no place like home!

...

To thee I'll return, overburdened with care;

The heart's dearest solace
will smile on me there;

No more from that cottage again will I roam;

Be it ever so humble, there's
no place like home.

Home! Home! Sweet sweet home!

There's no place like home!
There's no place like home!

John Howard Payne

IMAGE CREDITS

Have you enjoyed this book? If so, find us on Facebook at **Summersdale Publishers**, on Twitter at **@Summersdale** and on Instagram at **@summersdalebooks** and get in touch. We'd love to hear from you!

www.summersdale.com